REVIVAL SERMON OUTLINES

Books by Al Bryant

Climbing the Heights
Day by Day with C. H. Spurgeon
More Sermon Outlines for Special Occasions
More Sermon Outlines on Prayer
New Every Morning
Revival Sermon Outlines
Sermon Outlines for Evangelistic Occasions
Sermon Outlines for Funerals and Other Special Occasions
Sermon Outlines for Lay Leaders
Sermon Outlines on Bible Characters (Old Testament)
Sermon Outlines on Bible Characters (New Testament)
Sermon Outlines on the Attributes of God
Sermon Outlines on the Deeper Life
Sermon Outlines on the Cross of Christ
Sermon Outlines on the Life of Christ
Sermon Outlines on Prayer
Sermon Outlines on Prophetic Themes
Sermon Outlines for Special Occasions
Sermon Outlines for Worship Services
Sourcebook of Poetry

REVIVAL
SERMON
OUTLINES

compiled by

Al Bryant

kregel
PUBLICATIONS

Grand Rapids, MI 49501

Revival Sermon Outlines © 1992 by Al Bryant and published by Kregel Publications, a division of Kregel, Inc., P.O. Box 2607, Grand Rapids, MI 49501. All rights reserved.

Cover and book design: Alan G. Hartman

Library of Congress Cataloging-in-Publication Data

Revival Sermon outlines / compiled and edited by Al Bryant.
    p.   cm.
Includes index.
    1. Evangelistic sermons—Outlines, syllabi, etc.
I. Bryant, Al, 1926-

| BV3797.A1R48 | 1992 | 251'.02—dc20 | 91-41882 |
| | | | CIP |

ISBN 0-8254-2193-4

2 3 4 5 Printing/Year 96 95

Printed in the United States of America

CONTENTS

FOREWORD

A minister once prayed that the Lord would revive His church. "You're asking for the revival to start in the wrong place," the Lord told Him. "Get the revival fires burning in your members' homes and then your church will have a new glow."

The "revival sermon outlines" in this collection were chosen to accomplish just that purpose. Selected from many sources, they have been compiled to provide preachers with a rich resource of biblical and topical messages. They are designed as "spring boards for sermons" to start a progression of thought and serve as a framework for the preacher's own development of the subject.

AL BRYANT

TEXTUAL INDEX

8

A NEW CREATURE

If any man be in Christ, he is a new creature (2 Cor. 5:17).

It is important to understand what we are as Christians, not merely what we ought to be, or what we will be, but what we are. Our text declares what every Christian is. "If *any* man," no matter who, is a Christian, "he is a new creature."

I. **He Is New in His Relations to God.**
   A. New in his relation to the *law* of God.
      1. "He that believeth not is condemned already" (John 3:18).
      2. "There is therefore now no condemnation to them who are in Christ Jesus" (Rom. 8:1).
      3. The convict is pardoned, and becomes a new man in relation to the law.
   B. New in relation to the *government* of God.
      1. "Aliens from the commonwealth of Israel" have become "no more strangers and foreigners, but fellow-citizens with the saints" (Eph. 2:12, 19).
   C. New in relation to the *family* of God.
      1. Every Christian is "of the household of faith."

II. **If Any Man Be in Christ He Is New in His Relations to His Fellow-Man.**
   A. A new man in responsibility.
      1. "Now, then, we are ambassadors for Christ."
      2. "He hath committed unto us the word of reconciliation" (2 Cor. 5:19,20).
   B. New in opportunity.
      1. Before the Christian is an open door.
      2. He can minister to sinning, suffering, sorrowing humanity.

III. **If Any Man Be in Christ, He Is a New Creature in His Experiences.**
   A. There is an abiding consciousness of security.
   B. The Christian is blessed in the thought that he is on the right side.
   C. Hope is a precious element in this new experience.

D.   Communion with God refreshes the soul.

E.   The whole range of experience is touched by the indwelling Christ.

IV.   **If Any Man Be in Christ, He Is a New Creature at the Center of His Being.**

A.   This new life may be repressed and undeveloped, but if any man be in Christ, the new life has been begotten in his soul.

B.   This is fundamental—"Except a man be born again (or anew) he cannot see the kingdom of God."

V.   **What a Wonderful Newness Is Ours!**

A.   Seeing these things are so, what manner of men ought we to be?

B.   Surely when anyone unsaved comes to see what a Christian really is, he must desire to have these blessings, to be a new creature.

C.   The door is open.

D.   We as Christians must enter by faith into the riches of grace in Christ Jesus, and all shall be ours.

REVIVAL SERMONS IN OUTLINE

ALL THINGS

In Relation to the Lord Jesus

He is *before* all things (Col. 1:17)
By Whom are all things (Heb. 2:10)
For Whom are all things (Heb. 2:10)
Heir of all things (Heb. 1:2)
Preeminent in all things (Col. 1:18)
He will *fill* all things (Eph. 4:10)

RITCHIE

BELONGING TO CHRIST

And ye are Christ's (1 Cor. 3:23).

I. **Here Is Ownership, With the Idea of Responsibility.**
   We as believers are Christ's—
   A. By creation.
   B. By providence.
   C. By donation.
   D. By redemption.
   E. By conquest.
   F. By surrender.

II. **Here Is Relationship with the Idea of Privilege.**
   This relationship is expressed in various ways in the Scriptures.
   A. We are His sheep (John 10:1-15).
   B. We are His servants (Acts 4:29).
   C. We are His friends (John 15:13-15).
   D. We are His brothers (Matt. 12:48; Mark 3:35).
   E. We are His bride (John 3:29; Rev. 21:2).
   F. We are His body (Rom. 12:4,5; Eph. 4:15,16).
   G. We are one in spirit with Christ (1 Cor. 6:17).
   H. "It doth not yet appear what we shall be: but we know that when He shall appear, we shall be like Him, for we shall see Him as He is" (1 John 3:2).

REVIVAL SERMONS IN OUTLINE

CONVERSION

A New Attitude toward God, an Outward Change in the Life
The Act (1 Thess. 1:9; 1 Peter 2:24; Acts 26:18)
The Need (Matt. 18:3; Acts 3:19; Isa. 53:6)
The Motive (Acts 11:21; Hosea 14:8; Phil. 3:8)
The Hindrances (Acts 28:27; 13:8; John 6:66)

500 BIBLE SUBJECTS

BURDENS

Every man shall bear his own burden (Gal. 6:5).

Bear ye one another's burdens (Gal. 6:2).

Cast thy burden on the Lord (Ps. 25:22).

There is a threefold cord not easily broken. There is no contradiction, not the slightest discordance in these texts.

I. **God Has Ordained That Everyone Shall Bear a Burden.**

   A. Some burdens are inseparable; deliverance from them is impossible.

      1. The burden of sorrow visits alike the palace and the hut.
          Every man must bear that burden.
      2. Our responsibilities, our physical infirmities, the difficulties of work, we all must bear them.
          No one can carry them for us.

II. **There Are Loads We Can Help Others to Carry, and Thus Learn Sympathy.**

   A. There is a sense in which we can bear each other's burdens and trials.

      1. No man is beyond the reach of human sympathy.
      2. Often a light lift, a mere touch, helps us over sorrow marvelously.

   B. If we get faint with discouragement, let us take hold of Christ and He will help us to carry our burden.

III. **The Third Text Takes Us from Self-Help and Brotherly Help Up to the Divine Help.**

   A. God does not release us from performance of duty, but He will sustain us in doing it.

   B. The load will not crush us, God's love will carry us and our burden too.

   C. The most overwhelming burden in God's universe is sin!

   D. Jesus Christ bore that burden for us.

   THREE HUNDRED OUTLINES ON THE NEW TESTAMENT

CASUALTIES OF EASE

Amos 6:1-7

Introduction

In this Scripture we are brought face to face with a tragic situation existing in Israel, also with the faithfulness of the prophet of God.

Here is described a people "at ease in Zion" in the face of gravest dangers.

A. Their pride (vv. 1,2). They considered themselves "the chief of nations," they trusted in their relation to "the house of Israel," they rested in the strength of the "mountain of Samaria"—*but* they had about them examples of the nations which had been destroyed (v. 2).

B. Their presumption that they would never be called to judgment for their wickedness (v. 3).

C. Their indulgence in all manner of sensual pleasures and ease (vv. 4-6).

D. They were not grieved for the affliction of Joseph (v. 6)—had no concern for the interests of the Church of Christ or for the nation which was sinking into decay.

They were "at ease in Zion"—careless, indifferent, unconcerned, lukewarm, blinded by this "ease" to the presence of gravest dangers. Judgment came—they were "casualties of ease." How pertinent is this message to this day?

I. Consider the National Situation.

Nations are threatened from without by terrorism and instability, from within by corruption and disease. We are in danger of losing our glorious liberties through "ease."

II. Consider the General Church Situation.

The loss of moral force, the loss of prestige, the loss of spiritual power among the peoples of the world. It is an inner weakness—a love of ease. There is a form of worship without heart devotion. The substance of religion is lost in the shadow. The spirit is lost in the letter. "A form of religion, but denying the power thereof." Inability of the Church to challenge its membership to spiritual pursuits.

III. Consider the Local Church Situation.

"At ease in Zion." How difficult it is to stir us to consistent activity! We permit any trifling excuse to keep us from doing the work of God. We are torn with petty bickerings, hypocrisies; we are victims of selfishness, lovers of ease, unwilling to search our own hearts, or to have God search us to know our actual state before Him.

Hear God's Word—"*Woe* to them that are at ease in Zion!" Shall we heed His Word?

SELECTED

CHRISTIAN EXPERIENCE: Its Scope and Dimensions

For we are His workmanship, created in Christ Jesus
unto good works . . . (Eph. 2:10).

The soul's sublime experience is salvation by grace through faith in the Lord Jesus Christ. The fullness of this gracious experience has a wide scope.

I. This Experience Has the Upward Reach

"We are His workmanship." We become new creatures in Christ by the grace of God (2 Cor. 5:17). It is the work of God the Father. The experience is with the Father, the Lord Jesus Christ and the Holy Spirit. Faith must reach upward and take hold of the grace of God by faith.

II. This Experience Has the Inward Reach

"Created in Christ Jesus." In *conviction* the soul realizes it is in sin. In *repentance* it turns away from sin and by faith unto Christ. In *regeneration* the soul is made new in Christ and becomes a new creation with new hope, new desires, new thoughts, and new purposes, and new determinations.

III. This Experience Has the Outward Reach

"Unto good works." God has a purpose in salvation. The saved soul will reach out for others for Christ. It will desire to become a laborer with God for a lost world (1 Cor. 3:9).

SERMONS IN OUTLINE

THE CHRISTIAN RACE

1 Corinthians 9:24

I. **Three Classes.**
   A. Non-competitors (Phil. 3:18,19; Heb. 2:3).
   B. Failing competitors (1 Cor. 3:15).
   C. Winning competitors(2 Tim. 4:7,8).

II. **Conditions for Competition.**
   A. Must be a citizen (Eph. 2:19).
   B. Blameless (Rom. 8:1).
   C. Must offer himself (Rom. 12:1).
   D. Must be accepted (Eph. 1:6).

III. **Conditions in the Race.**
   A. He must start right (John 10:9).
   B. Keep to the course (John 14:6).
   C. Must strip (Heb. 12:1).

IV. **Causes of Failure.**
   A. Turning or backsliding (Ps. 78:9; Acts 7:39).
   B. Tripping or careless walking (John 11:10).
   C. Tired or weary walking (Mal. 1:13; Isa. 40:31).

TOOLS FOR THE MASTER'S WORK
J. ELLIS

OUR HOPE

The Christian's hope is not the uncertain thing of men, but the well-grounded expectation of that which God has prepared for and promised to His people.

It is Christ in them (Col. 1:27)
A Good Hope (2 Thess. 2:16)
A Living Hope (1 Peter 1:3)
A Purifying Hope (1 John 3:3)
A Blessed Hope (Titus 2:13)

RITCHIE

THE CHRISTIAN REVIVED

I. **The Need of Revival**
  A. We need to be revived daily to follow the way God would have us go (Ps. 119:37).
  B. We need to be revived in God's righteousness (Ps. 119:40).
  C. Also in faith (2 Tim. 1:5-6).
  D. And in the truth (2 Peter 1:13).
  E. In the joy of our salvation (Ps. 51:12).
  F. In the heart and spirit (Ps. 51:10).
  G. In the spirit of our mind (Eph. 4:23).
  H. For His name's sake (Ps. 143:2).

II. **How Revived**
  A. By the Holy Ghost (Titus 3:5; Acts 1:8; 1 Cor. 2:4).
  B. By God's Word (Ps. 119:50, 93; John 6:63; Ps. 19:7).

III. **Results of Revival**
  A. We rejoice in God (Ps. 85:6).
  B. We keep His Word (Ps. 119:88).
  We have:
  C. Spirit of Praise (Ps. 107:1-9; 103:1-5).
  D. Renewal of worship (Ezra 9:8-9).
  E. Victory in trouble (Ps. 138:7; 71:20).
  F. Spirit of prayer (Ps. 80:18).
  G. It keeps us in path of righteousness (Ps. 23:3).
  H. Gives us strength (Isa. 40:31; Ps. 103:5).
  I. Gives us comforts (Isa. 57:18).
  J. Restores health to the soul (Jer. 30:17).
  K. Comforts the sorrowful (Jer. 31:25).

IV. **Revival Conditional**
  A. We must be humble (Isa. 57:15; Ps. 34:18).
  B. We must be contrite (Matt. 5:4; Luke 15:20).
  C. We must return and confess sin (Hos. 5:14-15; 6:1,2).
  D. We must wait on God (Isa. 41:31).

W. FLINT JONES

THE CHRISTIAN'S LIGHT

Let your light so shine before men, that they may see your good works, and glorify your Father which is in heaven (Matt. 5:16).

Christ, the light of the world, says to His followers, "Ye are the light of the world." There is no real discrepancy between the two statements: the city is lit by lamps and yet it is the electricity that does it all.

I. **There Is First the Positive Injunction That Christians Are to Do Everything in Their Power to Make Sure That Their Light Shall Shine as Brightly as Possible.**

This is to be done:
- A. By the position we take up.
  1. A lamp on the floor will not send out its rays so widely as if it were suspended from the ceiling.
  2. The Christian should connect himself with the Church, let his light shine by joining the company of those who confess with their mouths the Lord Jesus.
- B. By the character which we form.
  1. Character is the most important thing in the world.
  2. There is no eloquence so powerful as a good man's life.
- C. By the exertions we make for the conversion of fellow men.
  1. By these we benefit ourselves; let a man tie up his hand so that it becomes motionless, and by and by it will become withered and powerless like the dead limb of a wind-blasted tree.

II. **Look at the Negative Side of This Injunction.**

A. We should remove everything that tends either to obscure or to hide our light, or which so affects it as to make it suggestive of ourselves rather than of God.
  1. We should get rid of the undue reserve by which multitudes are characterized.
  2. We must keep ourselves clear from all practical inconsistencies.
  3. We should avoid all self-display. The best style in writing is that which gives the thought with such transparency that the reader sees nothing else; and that is the noblest Christian character which shows the most of Christ.

THREE HUNDRED OUTLINES ON THE NEW TESTAMENT

THE CHRISTIAN'S RELATION TO THE WORLD

Born into the World (John 16:21)

Given Out of the World (John 17:6)

Delivered from the World (Gal. 1:4)

Crucified to the World (Gal. 6:14)

Not of the World (John 17:16)

A Stranger in the World (1 John 3:2)

Hated by the World (John 17:14)

500 BIBLE SUBJECTS

THE CHRISTIAN'S PLACE IN THE WORLD

Sent into the World (John 17:18; 20:21)

Preaching to the World (Mark 15:15)

The Light of the World (Phil. 2:15; Matt. 5:14)

Live Godly in the World (Titus 2:12)

Not Conformed to the World (Rom. 12:2; John 17:15)

Love Not the World (1 John 2:16; 2 Tim. 4:10)

Passing Through the World (1 Peter 2:11)

No Friendship with the World (James 4:4; 1:27)

500 BIBLE SUBJECTS

WHAT CHRIST DOES FOR HIS PEOPLE

He Quickens Them (John 5:25)—As the Life-Giver

He Saves Them (Matt. 1:21)—As the Savior

He Seals Them (Eph. 1:13)—As the Owner

He Leads Them (John 10:27)—As the Shepherd

He Helps Them (Heb. 2)—As the Priest

He Restores Them (1 John 2:1)—As the Advocate

He Comes for Them (John 14:3)—As the Bridegroom
500 BIBLE SUBJECTS

THE DEITY OF CHRIST

Proclaimed by the Father (Matt. 1:23; John 1:1)

Claimed by the Son (John 10:30; 5:21; Rev. 1:8)

Witnessed by the Spirit (Heb. 1:8; 1 Peter 3:15, R.V.)

Owned by Angels (Heb. 1:6; Rev. 5:11-12)

Confessed by Saints (John 20:28; Rom. 9:5)

Feared by Demons (Mark 5:7; James 2:19)

Manifested by His Works (Luke 7:20; John 5:36)
500 BIBLE SUBJECTS

CONFESSING CHRIST

Matthew 10:32

The text is greatly emphasized by the circumstances of its utterance.

I. The Object to Be Confessed.

A. Not our good works, church membership, or worthy desires and purposes.

B. Not some remarkable experience.

C. But Christ as our Savior and King, our trust in Him for pardon, and our obedience to Him as our Lawgiver.

II. To Whom the Confession Is to Be Made.

A. To Christ—the heart.

B. To men—"before men" (Rom. 10:9,10). Do not hesitate from any cause. Remember:

   1. Christ requires it.
   2. He knows all about you.
   3. He wants to use your confession.

III. The Manner of Confessing.

A. By words; "with the mouth confession is made unto salvation."

B. By acts; the ordinances and an upright life.

IV. The Promise to Those Confessing.

A. Confessed now, which means forgiveness, reconciliation and unspeakably rich blessings in the life that now is.

B. Confessed hereafter; received into glory; welcomed by the King in His beauty; "Come ye blessed of my Father."

V. How Simple the Requirement, How Wonderful the Reward!

REVIVAL SERMONS IN OUTLINE

A CRY FOR HELP

2 Chronicles 14:11

This text is the cry of souls in need. It is a cry out of distress. The Lord is ready to hear and help in the time of need.

I. The Source of Help.

"Our God." We come to times in life when it seems that only the Lord can help us. The Lord knows every trial, temptation, trouble and task of the human life and He is abundantly able to help us in every need. He stands ready to extend a helping hand in the time of sin, sorrow, suffering and defeat. He is the source of all power. He is mighty and merciful and will extend His might and mercy to needy man if he will only trust Him and call on Him.

II. The Call for Help.

"Help us." Too often we do not call on the Lord until we reach utter despair. We call on the Lord when Death lays his cold hands on our loved ones and the doctors can do no more. We call when sorrow is so heavy that we can no longer bear it and live. We too often wait for extreme circumstances to call on the Lord when we should seek His help from the first and all along the way. He will hear our call. He will help us when we need Him. He will abundantly bless. He will give strength and courage and supply every need of the soul of man.

III. The Reason for Help.

"For we rest on thee." The Lord expects us to believe in Him and trust Him and call on Him. We must abide in Him as the branch abides in the vine. He is the giver and sustainer of life and we must trust Him for every need. From Him comes every good and perfect gift, but we must rely on Him for the gifts. Depend on the Lord, trust Him, and He will sustain thee.

SERMONS IN OUTLINE

TWO MIGHTY INTERCESSORS

I. We have an Advocate with the Father—Jesus Christ the Righteous (1 John 2:1). He ever liveth to make intercession for us (Heb. 7:25).

II. The Spirit Himself maketh intercession for us, with groanings which cannot be uttered: He maketh intercession for the saints according to the will of God (Rom. 8:26,27).

TWELVE BASKETS FULL

DOUBLE TITLES GIVEN TO THE LORD JESUS

I.   The Author and Finisher of Our Faith (Heb. 12:2)

II. The Apostle and High Priest of Our Profession (Heb. 3:1)

III. The Shepherd and Bishop of Our Souls (1 Peter 2:25)

TWELVE BASKETS FULL

JUSTIFICATION

A New State before God, a Forensic Term

The Sinner's State (Rom. 3:9,10; Isa. 64:6).

God, the Justifier (Rom. 8:33; 4:25)

Christ's Death the Procuring Cause (1 Peter 3:18).

Grace the Spring (Rom. 3:24; Gal. 2:16-24).

Faith the Principle (Rom. 5:1; Acts 13:39).

Resurrection the Witness (Rom. 4:25; 5:18).

Works the Evidence (James 2:26; Titus 3:8).

500 BIBLE SUBJECTS

THE FAITHFUL SAYING

*This is a faithful saying, and worthy of all acceptation,
that Christ Jesus came into the world to save sinners:
of whom I am chief (1 Tim. 1:15).*

Paul had described his ordination in verse 12. He then went on to speak of the grace manifested in the call of such a person to the ministry (v. 13), and of the further grace by which he was sustained in that ministry.

I. How We Preach the Gospel.
    A. As a certainty. It is a "faithful saying." We do not doubt the truth of our message, or how could we expect *you* to believe it. We believe, and are sure, because:
        It is a revelation of God.
        It is attested by miracles.
        It bears its witness within itself.
        It has proved its power upon our hearts.
    B. As an everyday truth. It is to us a "saying" or proverb.
    C. As claiming your attention. "Worthy of all acceptation."
        You must believe it to be true.
        You must appropriate it to yourself.
        You ought to do so, for it is worthy of your acceptance.

II. What Gospel Do We Preach?
    A. The gospel of a person: "Christ Jesus."
        He is the anointed of God: "Christ."
        He is the Savior of men: "Jesus."
        He is God and Man in One Person.
        He died, and yet He lives forever.
    B. The gospel for sinners.
        For such Jesus lived and labored.
        For such He died and made atonement.
        For such He has sent the gospel of pardon.
        For such He pleads in heaven.
    C. The gospel of effectual deliverance. "To save sinners."
        Not to half-save them.
        Nor to make them savable.
        Nor to help them to save themselves.
        Nor to save them as righteous.

But to save them wholly and effectually from their sins.

III. Why Do We Preach It?

    A.   Because we have been saved by it.

    B.   Because we cannot help it, for an inward impulse compels us to tell of the miracle of mercy wrought upon us.

> Will you not believe a saying so sure?
> Will you not accept a truth so encouraging?
> Will you not come to a Savior so suitable?

- A visitor to Rome says, "I was struck with the frequency with which the priests and other exhibitors of church curiosities use the phrase, 'It is said'—*on dit*—when describing relics and rarities. They do not vouch for their being what they are reputed to be. 'It is said.' Are they ashamed of their curiosities? Do they thus try to satisfy their consciences? They do not express their personal belief; but—*it is said*. Not thus do gospel preachers speak. That which we have seen and heard declare we unto you."

  There's a powerful word in the text—it is the word "acceptation." It's all provided for you. It's very much like a supper. You'll find the table laid, and everything all ready. You're not expected to bring anything at all.

  I was once invited out to tea by a poor widow, and I took something in my pocket. But I'll never do it again. It was two cakes; and when I brought them out and laid them on the table, she picked them up and flung them out into the street, and said, "I asked you to tea; I didn't ask you to provide tea for me." And so with Christ; He asks, He provides, and He wants nothing but ourselves; and if we take aught else, He'll reject it. We can only sup with Him when we come as we are.

  Luther says, "Once upon a time the devil said to me, 'Martin Luther, you are a great sinner, and you will be damned!' 'Stop! Stop!' said I; 'one thing at a time; I am a great sinner, it is true, though you have no right to tell me of it. I confess it. What next?' 'Therefore you will be damned.' That is not good reasoning. It is true that I am a great sinner, but it is written, 'Jesus Christ came to save sinners'; therefore I *shall be saved*! Now go your way. So I cut the devil off with his own sword, and he went away mourning because he could not cast me down by calling me a sinner."

C. H. SPURGEON

THE FEET

By Nature:

    I.   Almost Gone (Ps. 73:2)

   II.   Running to Evil (Prov. 1:16)

  III. Running to Mischief (Prov. 6:18)

  IV. On the Dark Mountains (Jer. 13:16)

   V. Sunk in the Mire (Jer. 38:22)

  VI. Swift to Shed Blood (Rom. 3:15)

 VII. Slide in Due Time (Deut. 32:35)

By Grace:

    I.   Washed (John 13:10)

   II.   Kept (1 Sam. 2:9)

  III. Set Upon a Rock (Ps. 40:2)

  IV. Not to Be Moved (Ps. 66:9)

   V. Shod with the Gospel (Eph. 6:15)

  VI. Bringing the Gospel (Rom. 10:15)

 VII. Bruising Satan (Rom. 16:20)

TWELVE BASKETS FULL

SEVEN FELLOWSHIPS

Fellowship with the Father (1 John 1:3)
Fellowship of the Son (1 Cor. 1:9)
Fellowship of the Spirit (Phil. 2:1)
Fellowship in the Light (1 John 1:7)
Fellowship of Suffering (Phil. 3:10)
Fellowship in Service (Col. 4:7)
Fellowship in the Gospel (Phil. 1:3)

RITCHIE

GOD'S WORD

I. **What It Does for Me**
   A. Quickens me. "Quicken thou me according to Thy Word" (Ps. 119:25).
   B. Sanctifies me. "Sanctify them through Thy truth" (John 17:17).
   C. Cleanses me. "Wherewithal . . . according to Thy Word" (Ps. 119:9).

II. **What It Is to Me**
   A. Precious. "The word . . . was precious in those days" (1 Sam. 3:1).
   B. Penetrating. "Piercing even . . . soul and spirit" (Heb. 4:12).
   C. Powerful. "Like a hammer" (Jer. 23:29).
   D. Purifying. "Like as a fire" (Jer. 23:29).
   E. Protecting. "Sword of the spirit" (Eph. 6:17).

III. **How It Should Be Treated by Me**
   I am to:
   A. Love it. "How I love Thy law!" (Ps. 119:97).
   B. Search it. "Search the Scriptures" (John 5:39).
   C. Feed on it. "I did eat them" (Thy Words) (Jer. 15:16).
   D. Hold Fast to it. "Holding fast the faithful word" (Titus 1:9).
   E. Preach it. "Preach the word" (2 Tim. 4:2).
   F. Meditate on it. "I will meditate on Thy precepts" (Ps. 119:15).
   G. Delight in it. "I will delight in Thy statutes" (Ps. 119:16).
   BIBLE THEMES FOR BUSY WORKERS

GOD TEACHES GODLY LIVING

Deuteronomy 5:32,33

I. Encourages Israel to Obey God's Word (Deut. 5:32,33).

    A. Encourages complete, wholehearted, exact and continuous obedience (v. 32).

    B. Encourages through assuring of blessing (v. 33).

II. Promises His Blessing (Deut. 11:26,27).

Present (immediate) blessing.

III. Promises Curse (Deut. 11:26, 28).

Present (immediate) curse.

IV. Describes Judgment upon Ungodliness in Ephraim (Isa. 28:1-6).

    A. Judgment especially upon drunkenness (v. 1).

    B. Judgment because of pride, confidence of guilty ones (v. 1).

    C. Judgment despite temporary prosperity (v. 1).

    D. Judgment through others (v. 2).

    E. Judgment that is speedy, unexpected, costly (v. 4).

    F. Judgment that means disappointment, heartache, loss (v.4).

    G. Judgment that will differentiate (vv. 5,6).

V. Promises Woe upon Ungodly Living (Hab. 2:12).

    A. Woe despite apparent success.

    B. Woe especially upon violence (blood) and upon establishing iniquity.

WILLIAM MCCARRELL

GOOD WORKS

The Believer in Christ is:

Created unto good works (Eph. 2:10)
Furnished unto all good works (2 Tim. 3:17)
Careful to maintain good works (Titus 3:8)
Prepared unto every good work (2 Tim. 2:21)
Zealous of good works (Titus 2:14)
Rich in good works (1 Tim. 6:18)
A Pattern in good works (Titus 2:7)

RITCHIE

A GOLDEN CHAIN OF BLESSING

Bless the Lord, O my soul, and forget not all His benefits: Who forgiveth all thine iniquities; Who healeth all thy diseases; Who redeemeth thy life from destruction; Who crowneth thee with lovingkindness and tender mercies; Who satisfieth thy mouth with good things; so that thy youth is renewed like the eagle's (Ps. 103:1-5).

Notice seven things in these verses that the Psalmist blesses God for:

I. **Forgiveness.** All, not some of, the past sins forgiven, and not only so, but forgotten. In the eleventh chapter of Hebrews, where we have recorded what faith has done, there is not a single word about the failures of these Old Testament saints. Why is this? Because, in the tenth chapter, God had said, "Your sins and iniquities I will remember no more."

II. **Healing.** It is the privilege of the child of God to know, that He can, if He wills, heal us of all our bodily as well as spiritual diseases.

III. **Redemption.** Not only are our past sins forgiven, but we have deliverance from the *power* of sin, and soon from its *presence*.

IV. **Lovingkindness.** Some people will do a kindness out of mere benevolence, but there is no love with it; not so with our Father. Recently, we saw an advertisement of a certain paper, which said it was the brightest, biggest, and best. Whether it is so or not, it is not for us to say; but we do know this, that our Heavenly Father gives the brightest, biggest, and the very best He has to give to us. Hence, in speaking, we have to get all the adjectives we can to express in some measure what He gives. His love is *great* love; His kindness is *lovingkindness*; His mercy is *tender, great, plenteous,* and *everlasting*.

V. **Tender Mercies.** These are not doles of charity, but mercies given out of His loving, Fatherly heart, by virtue of His Son's work, and enjoyed in the Spirit.

VI. **Satisfaction.** One of the Puritans has said that "man's heart is a triangle, so that if the whole world were in it, there would be still three corners left unfilled." But the believer has the work of Christ to satisfy his *conscience*, the word of the Father to assure his *mind*, and the presence of the Holy Spirit to fill his *heart*, so that there is not a single corner unoccupied.

VII. Renewing. I remember a friend saying once, when going to a place to hold special meetings, "We are looking for a *revival*"; and I replied that it showed they were in a bad state, as the Christian should *live in a revival*. Our inward man is, or should be, renewed day by day, not only when an evangelist is holding special meetings.

F.E. MARSH

REVIVAL REVISITED

Psalm 85:6

I. The Necessity for Revival.
Spiritual feebleness.

II. The Agent by Whom Revival Is Effected.
Not man, but God. "Wilt *Thou*."

III. The Means of Securing Revival.
Prayer, combined with expectancy.

IV. The Result of Revival.
Joy. "That Thy people may rejoice in Thee."

SELECTED

REVIVAL IN THREE STAGES

"Revive *me*" (Ps. 138:7)
"Revive *us*" (Ps. 85:6)
"Revive Thy *work*" (Hab. 3:2)

This is God's order, and it must not be reversed.

RITCHIE

THE HAPPY AND THE UNHAPPY MAN

Psalm 1:1-6

Two characters are presented; the one is pronounced happy, and the other miserable. Three things are said to characterize *the good man*:

I. He Shuns Evil Companions

A. Here is a classification of the wicked; ungodly, sinners, scornful; that is, without God—opposed to God—and having contempt for God.

B. Here is a progression of depravity—walking, standing, sitting.

II. He Delights in the Word of God.

A. The word "law" here stands for divine revelation.

1. Show me a holy, God-fearing man, and I will show you one who loves the Bible.

2. And what a man loves he thinks about; and so we read, "In His law he meditates day and night."

III. He Is Like a Tree Planted.

A. He is like a tree in his growth.

1. "Consider the lilies, *how* they grow."

B. "A tree planted"—that is, a tree cared for.

1. Such a tree is fenced in to protect it from wild beasts.

2. It is staked to preserve it from the wind.

3. It is watered in the time of drought.

Three things are affirmed of *the wicked man*:

I. He Will Be Condemned in the Judgment.

A. "Shall not stand in the Judgment."

1. This does not mean that he will not be present; "for we shall all appear before the Judgment Seat of Christ"; but the word "stand" here is a law term, and means the same as to be "justified."

II. His Companionship with the Righteous Will Terminate.

A. "Nor sinners in the congregation of the righteous."

III. His End Will Be Destruction:

A. "The way of the ungodly shall perish."

B. How much that means we do not know, but it is a doom that Jesus wept over, and from which He dies to save us.

REVIVAL SERMONS IN OUTLINE

HOW TO OVERCOME TEMPTATION

There hath no temptation taken you but such as is common to man: but God is faithful, who will not suffer you to be tempted above that ye are able; but will with the temptation also make a way to escape, that ye may be able to bear it (1 Cor. 10:13).

The apostle has just been warning against too much self-confidence; he now speaks against the opposite faults, too much downheartedness and despondency.

I. There Is a Precise Correspondence Between Strength and Trial.

A. The temptation is proportioned to the power of resistance.

B. Do not think there is something hard and heavy and worse than all the past to come: the burden is made for the back.

II. The Very Same Divine Act Makes Both the Trial and the Way to Get Out of It.

A. God allows us to be tempted only in the way of testing us, and He points a way of escape.

1. We are never brought into a blind alley; it is a thoroughfare, and we can get out if we please; with the Egyptians on this side, and the sea on that, God will clear the waters of the deep to make a way.

III. This Must Be So Unless God Make Himself a Liar.

I wish to put it strongly. If it were not so, men would have a right to turn upon God and to say, "Thou hast deceived me."

God does not force His help upon us; but nothing will come to us that we shall not be able to baffle and beat, so long as we have His strength for ours.

THREE HUNDRED OUTLINES ON THE NEW TESTAMENT

JONAH: A JOURNAL OF GOD'S FORGIVENESS

Jonah 3:10; 4:9-11

The whole story of God's amazing mercy and forgiveness is set out clearly in the Book of Jonah. It is a story in two parts, as follows:

I. The Mighty Work of God in Bringing Men to Repentance.

God does not forgive until men confess and forsake their sins in genuine repentance. But He carries on a never-ending campaign to bring all men everywhere to repentance. Four things are told us in this Book of Jonah about God's campaign to bring men to repentance:

A. God exercises great forbearance with sinful men—He forbears with them until their sins often mount up to the heavens (1:1,2).

B. He sends a chosen messenger to warn men and call them to repentance (1:1,2; 3:1-4).

D. Finally, God puts great power and blessing upon His messenger, so that His call will prove effective in all men's hearts (3:1-9).

II. The Great Mercy and Grace and Forgiveness of God Bestowed Upon Repenting Souls.

The Scriptures tell us five things about this supreme transaction in mercy, when God forgave a whole heathen city, and brought it to sincere repentance:

A. God's forgiveness was extended the very moment that He saw the unmistakable signs of repentance (3:10).

B. His forgiveness came from His great compassionate heart, just as Jonah had predicted before he left Palestine (4:1-3).

C. God's forgiveness came in great contrast to Jonah's grudging spirit of unforgiveness, as shown by his grief for his gourd and his sincere wish that the repentant people of Nineveh might die in their sins (4:4-9).

D. God's forgiveness was made greater in importance by His expressed desire to save the innocent—the 120,000 children in Nineveh who were not old enough to know their right hand from their left, "and much cattle" (4:10,11).

E. Jesus later explained that God's forgiveness of the people of Nineveh would be in decided contrast to His final condemnation (in the judgment) of the Jews who rejected Him and refused to turn from their evil ways (Matt. 12:39-42).

SELECTED

FACE TO FACE WITH GOD

Amos 4:12

I. **Prepare!**
Get ready. Solemn exhortation. All our life to prepare. Are we prepared? Are we ready?

II. **There Is a God to Meet.**
Useless to say "There is no God."
A. "Thou fool, this night. . . ."
B. Danger of not reckoning on a hereafter. We get ready for our holidays but not for heaven or judgment.
C. We cannot ignore the summons of death.
D. We shall be speechless if we do not wear the wedding garment. "The ten virgins." Five prepared and five not prepared. We shall knock at a shut door.

III. **Why Be Anxious to Prepare?**
A. Brevity and uncertainty of life.
B. We know not what any hour may bring forth.
C. We hold no lease on our lives.
D. The summons will come to us all.
E. "Now is the accepted time."

J. ELLIS

FAITH

The Word of Faith (Rom. 10:8)—The Preacher's Message

The Hearing of Faith (Gal. 3:2)—The Hearer's Responsibility

The Obedience of Faith (Rom. 16:16)—The Receiver's Response

The Righteousness of Faith (Rom. 4:13)—The Believer's Position

The Walk of Faith (2 Cor. 5:6)—The Believer's Path

The Work of Faith (1 Thess. 1:3)—The Christian's Service

The Fight of Faith (1 Tim. 6:12)—The Soldier's Warfare.

RITCHIE

GENUINE REVIVAL: AN ENLIGHTENING LOOK

Luke 3:15-17

I.   An Interest on the Part of the People.
   A.   There are times when communities as well as individuals are ripe for the Gospel harvest.
   B.   Paul was permitted to preach in certain localities and forbidden to preach in other sections.

II.   A Spirit of Expectation.
   A.   On the part of the minister.
   B.   On the part of the people.

III.   A Spirit of Thoughtfulness.
Frivolity or lightness in either the pulpit or pew not conducive to a revival spirit.

IV.   The Hearts of the People Stirred.

V.   Holy Ghost Preaching.
   A.   Pungent conviction.
   B.   Genuine conversions.
   C.   Bible standard of holiness.

VI.   Spirit of True Humility.
"The voice of one crying in the wilderness."

VII.   Magnifying Christ.
   A.   He is greater than all preachers.
   B.   Larger than all our plans.
   C.   More powerful than all obstacles.

VIII.   Results of a True Revival.
   A.   Purging process (1 Peter 4:17).
   B.   Gathering of God's People.
      1.   Sound in doctrine.
      2.   Clear in experience.
      3.   Exemplary in their lives.

H. A. SHERWOOD

JOSEPH AND JESUS

I. Joseph, the Shepherd (Gen. 49:24)
    Joseph, Stripped (Gen. 37:23)
    Joseph, Sold (Gen. 37:28)
    Joseph, in the Pit (Gen. 37:24)
    Joseph, Falsely Accused (Gen. 39:14)
    Joseph, in Prison (Gen. 39:20)
    Joseph, Hated (Gen. 37:4)
    Joseph, Wept (Gen. 50:17)
    Joseph, Raised to the highest place in Egypt (Gen. 41:40)

II. Jesus, the Good Shepherd (John 10:11)
    Jesus, Stripped (Matt. 27:28)
    Jesus, Sold (Matt. 26:15)
    Jesus, in the Pit (Ps. 88:4)
    Jesus, Falsely Accused (Mark 14:56-57)
    Jesus, in Prison (Isa. 53:8)
    Jesus, Hated (John 15:24)
    Jesus, Wept (John 11:35)
    Jesus, Raised to the highest place in Glory (Eph. 1:20-21)

PEGS FOR PREACHERS

JUDGMENT

In Various Aspects

Judgment of the Sinner, Predicted (Heb. 9:27; Eccl. 11:9; 2 Peter 2:2-4; Heb. 10:27)

Judgment of the Believer, Past (John 5:24 R.V.; Rom. 8:1, 23-24; Gal. 2:20)

Judgment of the Servant, Future (2 Cor. 5:10; Rev. 22:12; Col. 3:24-25; 1 Cor. 4:1-5).

500 BIBLE SUBJECTS

THE JOY OF SALVATION

Psalm 51:12

This is called the Penitent Psalm. A careful study of it will reflect the past experience of the writer. He had done some great wrong. It will also betray the secret desire of the heart. It is filled with shame, remorse and concern. Let us see what the text reveals:

I. There Is Joy in Salvation.

A. There are two extreme views held about this. One is that salvation is a sane, cold-blooded, rationalistic thing, and one simply decides to quit some things and to begin doing other things. The opposite view is that salvation is all emotion, shouting, weeping, screaming. Both views are extreme.

B. Joy accompanies salvation, but it is no part of it, nor is it always final proof of it. There may be salvation without it, and there may be joy without salvation. Do not be confused.

C. Joy is the natural response in the human heart to some extended favor. It often finds expression in human relationships; when we accept Christ, and believe His promises, and realize the blessings that are ours, who could keep us from being happy?

II. The Joy May Be Lost.

A. That is what had taken place in the heart of the psalmist. His prayer is a sad confession of it.

B. In essence salvation and joy are far apart: Salvation is from God, and joy is the human response. Salvation is eternal—joy is transient. Salvation is not affected by anything; joy is affected by everything.

C. Joy is an unstable quality, rising, falling, overflowing and perishing utterly.

III. The Lost Joy May Be Regained.

A. For this the psalmist hungered and prayed.

B. But it cannot be found until the rubbish that covered it is removed, and the filth that stained it is taken away.

C. Joy is found in obedience, not rebellion. It is found in fellowship, not in discord. It is found in activity, not in negativity.

SELECTED

OUR HOPE

I. The Coming of the Lord Is:
   A. A saving hope (Rom. 8:24)
   B. A good hope (2 Thess. 2:16)
   C. A blessed hope (Titus 2:13)
   D. A joyful hope (Heb. 3:6)
   E. A living hope (1 Peter 1:3)
   F. A purifying hope (1 John 3:3)
   G. A hope of righteousness (Gal. 5:5)

TWELVE BASKETS FULL

THE LIPS

By Nature:
   I. Unclean (Isa. 6:5)
   II. Uncircumcised (Ex. 6:12)
   III. Flattering (Ps. 12:2,3)
   IV. Lying (Prov. 12:22)
   V. Dissembling (Prov. 26:24)
   VI. Contentious (Prov. 18:6)
   VII. Holding the Poison of Asps (Rom. 3:13)

By Grace:
   I. Opened (Ps. 51:15)
   II. Sinning Not (Job 2:10)
   III. Joyful (Ps. 63:5)
   IV. Praising (Ps. 119:17)
   V. Keeping Knowledge (Prov. 1:2)
   VI. Dispersing Knowledge (Prov. 15:7)
   VII. Giving Thanks (Heb. 13:15)

TWELVE BASKETS FULL

NECESSITY OF REVIVAL

Habakkuk 3:2

I. **In What Does Revival Consist?**

   A. In quickening believers to a higher life.

   B. In awakening the church to her divinely appointed mission. The church has been organized for the great work of saving souls. A church often forgets this and acts as though her mission was to please and entertain the world. A true revival always corrects this.

   C. In leading sinners to Christ.

II. **There Is an Absolute Necessity for Revival.**

   A. Nothing does more good to the church than revival. A revival heals breaches and restores harmony.

   B. It calls out all the strength of the church. In times of revival there are no drones in the church; she is "like an army with banners."

   C. The existence of the church depends on revival. If there were no more children born into the world, the world would soon come to an end; so churches must perish without converts.

   D. Revival is necessary because of its influence on the wicked. A real revival brings out the character of the wicked; they yield or rebel.

   E. Revival is necessary because of its influence on communities. In 1842, during the great revival in Boston, theaters and saloons were closed, and the churches were all filled. During the great revival in Ireland, the sale of strong drink was greatly diminished, and the number of criminals decreased.

III. **How May Revival Be Secured?**

   A. By the study of God's Word.

   B. By self-examination and forsaking of sin.

   C. By meditating much on the condition of the unsaved.

   D. By united and persevering prayer.

   E. By the faithful preaching of the Gospel.

REVIVAL SERMONS IN OUTLINE

THE LORD'S PEOPLE

Are described in the Word as:

    I.   A Chosen People (Deut. 7:6; 2:9)

   II. A Redeemed People (Ex. 15:13; Eph. 1:7)

  III. A Peculiar People (Deut. 14:2; Titus 2:14)

  IV. A Separated People (Ex. 33:16; John 15:19)

   V. A Holy People (Deut. 7:6; 1 Peter 1:15)

  VI. A Happy People (Deut. 33:29; John 15:11)

500 BIBLE SUBJECTS

NOTHING—ANYTHING—EVERYTHING

  I. Nothing
- A. With God nothing shall be impossible (Luke 1:37)
- B. Without Me you can do nothing (John 15:5)
- C. In nothing be anxious (Phil. 4:6 R.V.)
- D. Lacked nothing (Luke 22:35)

 II. Anything
- A. If you shall ask anything (John 14:14)
- B. You shall receive anything (James 1:7)
- C. Is anything too hard for the Lord? (Gen. 18:14)
- D. Did you lack anything? (Luke 22:35)

III. Everything
- A. In everything by prayer (Phil. 4:6)
- B. In everything give thanks (1 Thess. 1:18)
- C. I know that Thou canst do everything (Job 42:2)
- E. Let everything . . . Praise the Lord (Ps. 150:6)

TWELVE BASKETS FULL

LOVE TO CHRIST

"Lovest thou Me more than these?" *(John 21:15).*

A mild rebuke for a grievous sin. The threefold denial was followed by a thrice-repeated question; and a thrice-repeated confession of love.

   I. **It Was a Loving Question.**
       It showed that He desired Peter's restoration.

  II. **It Was a Natural Question.**
       No one is so worthy of love as Christ.

 III. **It Was an Important Question.**
       Everything else depended on it.

  IV. **It Was a Reasonable Question.**
       How little evidence of love Peter had given!

   V. **It Was a Searching Question.**
       "Lovest thou Me *more than these?*"

       These words are ambiguous. They may mean:
       A. More than thou lovest these fishing-nets? etc.
       B. More than thou lovest these companions?
       C. More than these other apostles love Me?
           Probably the last. Our love to Christ is to be pre-eminent.
                                                        SELECTED

THE LIVING ONE: CHRIST

The Living *Stone* on which we *build* (1 Peter 2:5)
The Living *Bread* on which we *feed* (John 6:51)
The Living *Way* by which we draw *near* (Heb. 10:20)
The Living *Priest* through whom we *worship* (Heb. 13:25)
The Living *Hope* for which we *wait* (1 Peter 1:3)

                                                        RITCHIE

THE LORD OUR KEEPER

I. **What He Keeps**
   A. The Spirit—The thoughts
   B. The Soul—The desires (1 Thess. 5:23)
   C. The Body—The actions
   D. The Lips—"Keep the door of my lips" (Ps. 141:3)
   E. The Feet—"He will keep the feet of His saints" (1 Sam. 2:9)

II. **From What He Keeps**
   A. From Trouble (Ps. 32:7)
   B. From the Evil (John 17:15)
   C. From Strife of Tongues (Ps. 31:20)
   D. From Danger (Ps. 91:4)
   E. From Stumbling (Jude 24)

III. **How He Keeps**
   A. By the Immutability of God (Mal. 3:6)
   B. By the Power (1 Peter 1:5)
   C. By the Faithfulness (2 Thess. 3:3)
   D. By the Mercy (Ps. 138:8)
   E. By the Love (Jer. 31:3)
   F. By the Word (Prov. 6:22)

BIBLE THEMES FOR BUSY WORKERS

THE LORDSHIP OF CHRIST

Exalted as Lord (Acts 2:36; Phil. 2:9-10)

All Authority given Him (Matt. 28:18; John 17:2)

Confessed Lord in Conversion (Rom. 10:9)

Sanctified Lord in the Heart (1 Peter 3:15)

Owned as Lord in the Life (Col. 3:17)

Acknowledged Lord in the Church (1 Cor. 14:37)

To be Honored as Lord by all (Phil. 2:10)

RITCHIE

THE MERCHANT

*The merchandise of it is better than the merchandise of
silver, and the gain thereof than fine gold (Prov. 3:14).*

This is one of the most forceful and impressive of all the proverbs
of Solomon. He takes a merchant who traffics in silver and gold to
set forth the reality and activities of religion. The holy experience of
grace and Christ's righteousness in the soul is as much of a reality as
silver and gold is real.

   I. The Analogy.
       A. The merchant wisely locates his business for success.
           1. So the Christian will first locate his gifts of prayer,
               song, strength, and whatever God has given him for
               service.
       B. The wise merchant fills his place with goods for sale.
           1. The Christian for happiness and usefulness will see
               to it that his heart is filled with holy experience,
               grace and truth.
       C. The successful merchant advertises his business to the
world.
           1. The Christian will likewise ever be ready to give his
              testimony to win souls.
       D. The merchant has great concern about the prices of
goods and general state of the market.
           1. The child of God will in like manner have deep
               interest about the affairs and state of Zion.
       E. The retail merchant keeps up a frequent correspondence
with the great trading marts.
           1. So with the faithful Christian.
           2. He will be constant in prayer, and have
               correspondence with the divine Lord.
       F. Merchants differ in talents, some with large and some
with smaller gifts.
           1. So with Christians; but all are to give service to the
               best of their ability.
       G. The successful merchant accommodates himself to his
customers.
           1. The faithful Christian will always be on the alert to

suit his words, acts, and influence to the best good of those around him.

H. A good merchant both dispenses and receives benefits.
   1. He sells for the benefit of others, and receives profits himself.
   2. So the useful Christian—he gives blessings to others and thereby receives benefit to his own soul.

I. The successful merchant closes up his life work with large gain.
   1. How many earnest and faithful Christians will have their crowns bedecked with stars, and yet walk the golden streets with those they have led to Christ.

II. The Application.

Will everyone who hears this discourse enter at once into holy traffic for Jesus as you never have before?

REVIVAL SERMONS IN OUTLINE

THE RESULTS OF THE NEW BIRTH

   I. Likeness.
      "The image of Him that created him" (Col. 3:10).

  II. Knowledge.
      "Renewed in knowledge" (Col. 3:10).

 III. Hatred of Sin.
      "Doth not commit sin" (1 John 3:9).

  IV. Victory.
      "Overcometh the world" (1 John 5:4).

   V. Love to All Saints.
      "We love the brethren" (1 John 3:14).

CHARLES INGLIS

THE MERCY OF THE LORD

As God had mercy on Nineveh, so He has had mercy upon us. It is for us to believe in, and accept His mercy, by accepting Christ.

Think of the character of His mercy.

I. **His mercy is great** (Num. 14:18; Ps. 103:11; 145:8). It is great, because the Father is the Source of it; it is great, because of the price it cost before it could reach us, for sin had blocked up the way. The cost was the blood of Christ.

II. **His mercy is enduring** (1 Chron. 16:34, 41; 2 Chron. 5:13; 7:3, 6; 20:21; Ps. 106:1; 107:1; 118:1; 136:1 to the end; and Jer. 33:11). Having put His hand to the plough, He never looks back.

III. **His mercy is plenteous** (Ps. 86:5, 15; 103:8). He does not dole it out grudgingly, but showers it upon us abundantly.

VI. **His mercy is tender** (Luke 1:78). He has mercy upon us, not as a judge, but as a Father.

V. **His mercy is rich, or He is rich in mercy** (Eph. 2:4). He keeps not the riches of His mercy to Himself, but, like Joseph, who gave of his abundance to his brethren, even so the Lord gives us of His fullness.

VI. **His mercy is saving** (Titus 3:5). We should never have been saved if our salvation had depended upon ourselves; but He held out the scepter of mercy to us, as Ahasuerus did to Esther.

VII. **His mercy is abundant** (1 Peter 1:3). It is not like a brook that dries up in the summer, but like the sea, which is unlimited. His mercy shall be as an attendant to accompany us (Ps. 23:6), and as an army to encompass us (Ps. 32:10).

F. E. MARSH

NEEDLESS CARE

"Be careful for nothing" (Phil. 4:6).

Some may question the reasonableness of this exhortation. Man is a thinking animal, and the more he advances in civilization the more provident he becomes.

I. **What This Exhortation Allows.**
   A. Watchfulness over our daily conduct.
   B. Regard to our eternal welfare.
   C. Solicitude for the welfare of others.

II. **What the Exhortation Forbids.**
   A. Undue anxiety about our temporal prospects.
   B. Fear respecting the success of the Gospel.
   C. Restlessness about matters beyond our control.

III. **Why the Exhortation Was Given.**

   Because the needless care:
   A. Destroys our peace.
   B. Interferes with the discharge of present duty.
   C. Ruffles the temper.
   D. Makes us troublesome to our neighbors.
   E. Leads to rashness.
   F. Indicates distrustfulness.
   G. Is altogether unprofitable.

IV. **Why the Exhortation Should Be Obeyed.**

   Because:
   A. We are ignorant of the future.
   B. God is in charge.
   C. Confident Christians are a credit to their Father.
   D. Knowing God is the highest knowledge.

SEEDS AND SAPLINGS

NO CONDEMNATION

There is therefore now no condemnation to them which are in Christ Jesus, who walk not after the flesh, but after the Spirit (Rom. 8:1).

The truth here declared follows from the position taken up by Paul in the preceding portion of his epistle.

I. **There Is No Condemnatory Sentence in Execution Against Christians Now.**

   A.   Believers in Jesus Christ still sin, and their sins are noticed by God, and God is displeased with them; but He does not treat them as criminals, but as children.

      1.   No sentence of condemnation is being executed outwardly and none is being executed inwardly.
      2.   Being justified by faith we have peace with God.

II. **There Is No Sentence of Condemnation Recorded for Execution.**

   A.   The disciple of Christ is not reproved but pardoned, and his pardon is full and complete.

      1.   In God's book there is no recognition whatever of the sins He has forgiven.
      2.   He does not throw our sins on the surface of the sea to appear again like bread cast on the waters, but buries them in the depths.

III. **The Absence of All Condemnation Is Accounted for by That Which Christ Is to the Soul That Relies Upon Him.**

   A.   Christ is the Lamb of God that takes away the sin of the world.

      1.   Simple trust appropriates the sin-offering.

   B.   He is the High Priest who ever lives to make intercession for us, and faith in Jesus gives us a personal interest in that intercession.

   C.   But how may I know whether I am trusting the true Christ, the Christ of God?

      1.   The reality of our reliance on the Christ of God is proved by the character and style of our life.
      2.   Jesus Christ leads all His disciples to walk not after the flesh but after the Spirit.

THREE HUNDRED OUTLINES ON THE NEW TESTAMENT.

THE PARABLE OF THE NET

Again, the kingdom of heaven is like unto a net ... (that) gathered of every kind: which, when it was full, they drew to shore, and sat down, and gathered the good into vessels, but cast the bad away... (Matt. 13:47, 50).

The parables of Jesus were calculated to interest all classes of persons: the laborer, the sower, the shepherd, and the fisherman. All had divine truth brought down to their understanding, and illustrated by the peculiarities of their several employments. In this parable the Savior represents the kingdom of heaven as like unto the net which being cast into the sea, encloses within it all kinds of fish. When it is full and brought to shore, the good are separated from the bad. So, says the Great Teacher, shall it be at the end of the world. The angels shall come forth and sever the wicked from among the just, etc. (vv. 49,50). Observe,

I. *The State in Which Men Are by Nature.*

In the world, represented in the parable by the sea. The world as distinguished from the Church, like the sea is an element of restlessness and peril. A state of imminent danger to the best interests of the soul. In this state all unconverted men are found. Hence as the sea abounds with fish of every kind, so the world with sinners of all descriptions. Here are all the various grades of moral evil—from the self-righteous moralist to the vilest profligate, or daring blasphemer.

II. *Observe the Only Means of Extricating Men Is by the Gospel.*

This is the net of the parable. Just as the net is adapted to enclose the fish in the sea, so is the gospel to save sinners.

A. *It comes down to their circumstances of moral wretchedness.* It recognizes them as fallen and perishing, and it contemplates their deliverance. It announces their ruin, and proclaims their help. It asserts their disease, and offers the healing balm.

B. *It is adapted to the circumstances of all sinners.* Like a large drag-net, it comprehends in its designs the rescue of all men. It embraces the wide world. It is addressed to every creature. It speaks to man as man, and reveals a Savior to every perishing sinner. Hence the commission given by Christ to the disciples (Mark 16:15).

C. *The gospel exclusively is adapted to save sinners*. It is God's expedient, and replete with His unerring wisdom. It is the power of God to salvation to every one that believeth. Faith cometh by hearing it, and salvation through faith. We know of no other means of men obtaining justification, holiness, and eternal life.

III. *The Gospel Must Be Connected with Active Instrumentality.*

Thus the net must be employed. It must be cast into the sea. So the gospel must be preached. How can men hear without a preacher? Observe,

A. *God has appointed the Christian ministry for this end.* He called, qualified, and sent forth the apostles and evangelists to cast this net into the sea. To preach the gospel. He does so still. He raises up holy, benevolent, and zealous ministers to give themselves earnestly and devotedly to fishing for souls. Jesus says now, as in the days of His flesh. "Follow Me, and I will make you fishers of men." Observe,

B. *That preaching the gospel is an arduous, laborious work.* Few occupations involve more toil and fatigue, and self-denial, than that of the fisherman. Such also is the laborious calling of the Christian minister. He must be wholly given to it in heart, and holy desire for the good of souls. Instant in season and out of season. He must sacrifice the love of ease, and the honors and rewards of the world, and bear the cross of his Divine Master. He must tread in the self-denying steps of his blessed Lord. He must not shun to declare the whole counsel of God. He must bear the truth to men under all circumstances and at all hazards. The early preachers of the cross, as well as modern missionaries, hazarded their lives for Christ and His cause. Observe,

IV. *That the Gospel Cannot Possibly Be Preached in Vain.*
"The net cast into the sea gathered of every kind" (v. 47).

Hence the intentions of the fisherman were answered. He did not empty his net in vain. So God has engaged that His Word shall not return unto Him void (Isa. 55:10,11). The success of the gospel has been varied. Sometimes multitudes of men have been converted, as on the day of Pentecost. During the ministry of Wesley and Whitfield, and others. But in all ages and countries, where the cross has been lifted up, sinners have been drawn out of the world to Christ. It is so now, both in our own and in heathen lands. It shall be very successfully so, introductory to the millennial reign of the Savior (see Isa. 60:7,8, etc.). Notice,

V. *That All Brought into Christ's Visible Church Are Not Converted Persons.*

The net enclosed "of every kind." Not only will the gospel save men of all ranks and ages, and conditions, but it will bring many into the outward kingdom of Christ, who are not regenerated, spiritual persons. Good and bad.

    A. Many hypocrites, as Judas, Ananias, and Sapphira, etc.

    B. Many formalists, having only a name to live, etc.

    C. Many inconsistent. Who run well for a season, but who are hindered, etc. Who make shipwreck, etc.

VI. *That in the Day of Judgment There Will Be a Complete Separation of the Righteous and the Wicked* (see vv. 48,49).

    A. The period certified is when the net is full and brought to shore. When the gospel dispensation is consummated. The end of the world.

    B. The agency is that of angels, the ministers of the divine judgments. See parable of the wheat and tares (v. 39).

    C. The scrutiny will be exact. All the good will be gathered out. Every sincere believer will be recognized and exalted. Every hypocrite and unconverted person will be detected. Escape will be impossible.

    D. The decision to the ungodly will be awful and final. "Cast away." "Cast into the furnace of fire," etc. (v. 30). Without hope—the subjects of weeping and wailing, and gnashing of teeth.

    E. The salvation of the righteous will be certain. "Happy the people in such a case," etc.

JABEZ BURNS

PASSION FOR SOULS

Jeremiah 20:9

Passion for souls is the rarest of all Christian virtues.

I. **It Is Kindled in the Soul of the Believer:**
   A. By the conviction that a divine commission or dispensation of the Gospel is committed to him (Jer. 1:17; 1 Cor. 9:17).
   B. By a consciousness of a debt owed to humanity (Rom. 1:14; 1 Thess. 2:4); we are debtors to man and trustees of the Gospel.
   C. By the hearty persuasion of the truth of the message, i.e., the terrors of the Lord, and the love of Christ (2 Cor. 5:11, 14).
   D. By self-sacrifice for others' sakes (Rom. 9:1-3; 10:1; Col. 1:24).
   E. By confidence in the redeeming power of God's Gospel (Isa. 55:11; 1 Tim. 1:16).

II. **Its Effects in the Character and Life:**
   A. Overcoming natural self-distrust, slowness of speech, etc. (Jer. 1:4-9).
   B. Boldly meeting antagonism and ridicule (Eph. 6:19,20).
   C. Creating an inward necessity. Pent-up fire (Ps. 39:3; Matt. 12:34; Acts 4:20).
   D. Imparting courage to attempt to save even the chief of sinners. Passion for souls awakening hope for them.
   E. Becoming the secret of actual uplifting power. Men cannot resist impassioned earnestness. There is no logic like that of love.

A. T. PIERSON

TRUE REVIVAL: Its Indications

Ezekiel 37:7

In this and the succeeding verses we may trace the indications of a true revival. We have here:

   I.   **The Declaration of the Truth.**
"So I prophesied as I was commanded."

  II.   **The Effect Produced.**
"There was a noise."

 III.   **The Visible Effect.**
"And behold a shaking."

 IV.   **The Visible Effect Takes a Particular Form.**
"And the bones came together."

  V.   **The Holy Ghost Is Manifested and Life Is Given.**
See verses 9 and 10.

SERMONS IN OUTLINE

THE VICTOR'S CROWN

I will give the a crown of life (Rev. 2:10).

   I.   The Christian's Reward Is Glorious—"A crown."

  II.   The Christian's Reward Is Durable—"A crown of life."

 III.   The Christian's Reward Is Personal—"I will give Thee."

PULPIT GERMS

PRECIOUS P'S

1 John 3:1-3

   I.   Priceless Privilege (v. 1)

  II.   Positive Promise (v. 2)

 III.   Purifying Power (v. 3)

GLEANINGS

PAUL'S THREE MEN

1 Corinthians 2:14; 3:1

I. The Natural Man (1 Cor. 2:14).
   A. He is not a converted man (1 Peter 1:23)
   B. He may be a religious man (James 1:26).
   C. He may be an educated man (Acts 22:3).
   D. He is dead in sins (Eph. 2:1).
   E. He has no spiritual life (Eph. 4:17,18).
   F. He has no spiritual discernment (1 Cor. 2:14).
   G. He is without God and without hope (Eph. 2:12).

II. The Carnal Man (1 Cor. 3:1-4).
   A. He may be a Christian (1 Cor. 1:2 with 3:1).
   B. He is like a child (1 Cor. 3:1).
   C. He never advances spiritually (1 Cor. 3:2).
   D. He follows the way of the flesh (Rom. 8:7; 1 Cor. 3:3).
   E. He is conformed to the world (Rom. 12:2).
   F. He causes division in the church (1 Cor. 1:10-13; 3:4).
   G. He produces the fruit of carnality (Heb. 5:11-14).

III. The Spiritual Man (1 Cor. 2:9-16).
   A. He is led by the Spirit (Rom. 8:14).
   B. He is not of the world (John 17:16).
   C. He is not understood by the world (1 John 3:1).
   D. He has the mind of Christ (Phil. 2:5).
   E. He seeks God's deeper things (Ps. 1:2; 1 Cor. 3:1,2).
   F. He is able to overcome the world (1 John 5:4,5).
   G. He is producing the fruit of the Spirit (Gal. 1:16-22).

Conclusion:
   A. We are one of the three classes.
   B. We should ask ourselves where we are.
   C. We should seek to be out-and-out for Christ.

C. C. MAPLE

THE SEVEN CHURCHES

A History of the Entire Church Through the Ages
Revelation 2, 3

   I. Ephesus, the Church in *Early Purity*.

  II. Smyrna, the Church in *Persecution*.

 III. Pergamos, the Church united with the *World*.

 IV. Thyatira, *Romanism* ruling supreme.

  V. Sardis, *Protestantism*.

VII. Laodicea, the *World-Church*.
     The last four go on together until the end.

500 BIBLE SUBJECTS

THE CHRISTIAN STEWARDSHIP

   I. The Master's Appointment (Matt. 25:14; Mark 13:34)

  II. The Steward's Responsibility (1 Cor. 4:1-3; 2 Tim. 2:2)

 III. The Trust Committed (1 Thess. 2:4; 2 Tim. 1:14)

     The Gospel for all (Mark 15:15; Rom. 1:4)
     The Truth, all of it (Matt. 28:20; Acts 20:27)

 IV. The Steward's Character (Titus 2:7; 1 Cor. 4:2)
     A Good Steward (1 Peter 4:10)—Dispensing
     A Wise Steward (Luke 12:42)—Discriminating
     An Unjust Steward (Luke 16:1)—Wasting

  V. The Reckoning Day (2 Cor. 5:9; 1 Cor. 4:5)

RITCHIE

REVIVAL: Keys to the Concept

Introduction:
- A. This text is often used to urge prayer for a revival.
- B. Primarily it is a promise to sinners.
- C. Secondarily, however, it contains a number of factors essential to a spiritual awakening.

I. **A Revival Is Not a Cause, but a Result.**
- A. Physical achievement means compliance with physical laws:
  1. Gravity.
  2. Attraction.
  3. Inertia.
  4. Leverage.
- B. Mechanical results come from use of mechanical means.
- C. Spiritual results come from compliance with spiritual laws.
  1. To produce spiritual results, one must use spiritual means.

II. **A Revival Is the Result of Co-operative Effort.**
- A. There must be effort on God's part.
  1. But all is not dependent on God.
  2. It is possible for us to limit the Holy One of Israel.
- B. There must be effort on man's part.
  1. A factor is your praying about a revival.
  2. A factor is your preparation for a revival.
  3. A factor is your enthusiasm concerning a revival.
  4. A factor is your presence at a revival.
  5. A factor is your effort during a revival.

E. S. PHILLIPS

THINGS TO "HOLD FAST"

The Name (Rev. 2:13)
The Word (Titus 1:9)
The Hope (Heb. 10:23)
That which is good (1 Thess. 5:21)
How?—"In Faith and Love" (2 Tim. 1:13)
How Long?—"Till I Come" (Rev. 2:25)

RITCHIE

REVIVALS OF RELIGION

Isaiah 60:8

I.   At some future time a vast multitude of mankind will be gathered unto the church of Christ.

II. This multitude will, in a great measure, consist of such persons as were not rationally expected to become Christians.

III. These persons will enter the church of their own accord, and with great earnestness of mind.

IV. They possess a dove-like character.
Remarks:
From these observations it is evident that there will hereafter be a general revival of religion in the world, which will furnish a solid foundation of joy to the universe.

The same things are partially true of every revival of religion.

We are bound faithfully to labor, and fervently to pray for the increased revival of religion.

REVIVAL SERMONS IN OUTLINE

THOSE WHO SEEK THE LORD

Isaiah 55:6

I.   They Shall Find God and Live (Deut. 4:29; Jer. 29:13).

II.   They Shall Rejoice (Ps. 40:16; 70:4; 105:3).

III. They Shall Understand (Prov. 28:5).

IV.   They Shall Not Want (Ps. 23:1).

V.   They Shall Not Be Confounded (Ps. 69:6).

VI.   They Shall Not Be Forsaken (Ps. 9:10).

VII. They Shall Be Blessed (Ezra 8:22).

VIII. They Shall Be Greatly Rewarded (Heb. 11:6).

TREASURES OF BIBLE TRUTH

REVIVAL'S REQUIREMENTS

You desire an outpouring of the Holy Spirit in your church? Four conditions must be observed. They are essential—mark the word, essential.

A. Is there any sin in your past that you have not confessed to God? On your knees at once! Your past must be put away and cleansed.

B. Is there anything in your life that is doubtful? Away with it! There must not be a trace of a cloud between you and God. Have you forgiven everyone? If not, don't expect forgiveness of your own sins; you will not get it (Matt. 6:12; Mark 11:25,26).

C. Do what the Spirit prompts. Obedience—prompt, implicit, unquestioning obedience to the Spirit. Better offend ten thousand friends than quench the Spirit of God.

D. A public confession of Christ as your Savior. There is a vast difference between profession and confession.

You praise the Father, praise the Son; why do you not praise the Holy Spirit? You speak of Him as "something!" The Spirit has been smothered in hundreds of our churches. Quench not the Spirit (1 Thess. 5:19). When the fire burns, it purifies, and when purified, you are useful in the work of God.

EVAN ROBERTS

A SIXFOLD BLESSING IN ROMANS 5

I. Peace. "Peace with God" (v. 1).
II. Position. "Access by faith" (v. 2).
III. Privilege. "We joy in God" (v. 11).
IV. Path. "Tribulations" (v. 3).
V. Power. "By the Holy Ghost" (v. 5).
VI. Preservation. "Saved by His life" (v. 10).

CHARLES INGLIS

SAINTS IN WRONG PLACES

  I. **A Discouraged Worker**
      Elijah under a juniper tree (1 Kings 19:4)

 II. **A Backsliding Believer**
      Abraham in Egypt (Gen. 12:10)

III. **A Disobedient Servant**
      Jonah in the sea-monster (Jonah 2)

 IV. **A Seduced Prophet**
      The man of God in the old prophet's house (1 Kings 13:19)

  V. **A Lazy Saint**
      David on the house-top (2 Sam. 11:2)

 VI. **A Silenced Witness**
      Lot in Sodom (Gen. 14:12)

VII. **A Miserable Disciple**
      Peter before the fire (Luke 22:65)

TWELVE BASKETS FULL

SALVATION

Threefold—Past, Present, Future

Past—From Sin's Penalty (Rom. 1:16; 10:10; Acts 28:18; 16:31; 1 Cor. 15:2; 2 Tim. 1:9)

Present—From Sin's Power (Heb. 7:25; Rom. 5:9; James 1:23; 1 Tim. 4:6; Phil. 2:12)

Future—From Sin's Presence (Rom. 13:11; Heb. 9:28; Phil. 3:20; 1 Thess. 5:8)

The *First* is immediate, secured by Christ's *Death*

The *Second* is continuous by Christ's *Life*

The *Third* is prospective at Christ's *Coming*

500 BIBLE SUBJECTS

SEVEN MARKS OF A CHRISTIAN

I. A Christian is a person who is Born Again: "Born again, not of corruptible seed, but of incorruptible, by the Word of God, which liveth and abideth forever" (1 Peter 1:23).

II. A Christian is a person who doesn't seek for Salvation Through Works: "Not of works, lest any man should boast" (Eph. 2:9); "God imputeth righteousness without works" (Rom. 4:6).

III. A Christian is a person who shows by works that he or she has got Salvation Through Christ: "Who gave Himself for us, that He might redeem us from all iniquity, and purify unto Himself a peculiar people, zealous of good works" (Titus 2:14).

IV. A Christian is one who Builds on a Sure Foundation: "Other foundation can no man lay than that is laid, which is Jesus Christ" (1 Cor. 3:11).

V. A Christian is a person who Confesses Christ among his fellows: "With the mouth confession is made unto salvation" (Rom. 10:10).

VI. A Christian is one who Serves the Lord Jesus and Waits for His Coming: He has "turned to God from idols to serve the living God, and to wait for His Son from Heaven" (1 Thess. 1:9,10).

VII. A Christian is a one who Carries the Message of Salvation to others and beseeches men, saying: "We pray you in Christ's stead be ye reconciled to God" (2 Cor. 5:20).

1,000 SUBJECTS FOR SPEAKERS AND STUDENTS

SEVEN THINGS CHRISTIANS SHOULD DO

They should live:

    I. A Life of Holiness (1 Thess. 5:22; 2 Tim. 2:19).

   II. A Life of Prayer (1 Tim. 2:8; 1 Thess. 5:17).

  III. A Life of Death (Heb. 11:6; Col. 1:23).

  IV. A Life of Self-Denial (Matt. 5:29; Gal. 5:24).

   V. A Life of Separation from the World (Ex. 32:26).

 VI. A Life of Consecration (Ex. 28:40-41; Rom. 12:1).

VII. A Life of Service (Deut. 10:12; Luke 16:13).

SEED BASKET

SOUL WINNING

Proverbs 11:30

Our prayer (Acts 6:6)

Our field (Mark 5:19,20)

Our time (Matt. 21:28)

Our motive (2 Cor. 5:14)

Our helper (John 15:5)

Our theme (John 3:16)

Our message (Rom. 1:16)

Our power (Acts 1:8)

Our example (Luke 2:49)

Our reward (2 Tim. 4:18)

SELECTED

SEVEN CHARACTERISTICS OF
THE PEOPLE OF GOD

I. **Characteristics**
   A. Disciples—In the same school—One Master (Acts 20:7)
   B. Children—In the same family—One Father (John 11:52)
   C. Sheep—In the same flock—One Shepherd (John 10:16)
   D. Saints—In the same covenant—One rank (Rom. 1:7)
   E. Stones—In the same house—One foundation (1 Peter 2:5)
   F. Members—In the same body—One Head (Rom. 12:5)
   G. The Bride—In the same glory—One Bridegroom (Rev. 21:2, 9)

II. **Application**
   A. All believers are alike disciples, though some have not made the same progress as others.
   B. All are alike children, sharing the same life, though some of them are mere babes, others young men or fathers in growth.
   C. All are alike sheep, though some follow the Shepherd more closely, listening to His voice.
   D. All are alike saints by calling, though some are more practically holy in their walk and conversation than others.
   E. All are alike living stones upon the one foundation, though some are more prominent in the building than others.
   F. All are alike members of the body, though some have a more honorable place and office than others.
   G. All will be together in the same glory, though some will suffer loss through unfaithfulness when in the body.

TWELVE BASKETS FULL

SIN: MEN MOCK BUT GOD HA

I. **What the Natural Heart Thinks of Sin.**
    A. Men sin easily. It is the natural flow of th
    B. They bear the load lightly, at ease in Zio
    C. The heavier the load, the more easily the
    D. The natural heart frequently excuses sin, blames it on the force of circumstances, etc.

II. **What God Thinks of Sin.**
    A. He hates it (Jer. 44:4).
    B. He has banished it from heaven and prepared perdition for it.
    C. He has punished it in His Son.

III. **What Awakened Souls Think of Sin.**
    A. Those converted on the day of Pentecost.
    B. The jailer. Sin has a sting (Rom. 7:9).

IV. **What Believers Think of Sin.**
    It is their plague—their enemy. Like God they hate it. Sometimes it grieves them. They long for the time when they shall be free from it, leaving it behind them forever.

PULPIT THEMES

SPIRITUAL REVIVAL

Wilt thou not revive us again: that Thy
people may rejoice in Thee? (Ps. 85:6).

Written at a time of religious awakening, such as took place in the reign of Jehoshaphat.

I. **The Necessity for Revival.**
    Spiritual feebleness.

II. **The Agent by Whom Revival Comes.**
    Not man, but God. "Wilt *Thou.*"

III. **The Means of Securing Revival.**
    Prayer, combined with expectancy.

IV. **The Result of Revival.**
    Joy. "That Thy people may rejoice in Thee."

OUTLINES OF SERMONS

TEMPTATION: How to Handle It

I. **You Can't Avoid It.**
   A. But you can avoid experiences that bring it on.

II. **How Should You Meet It?**
   A. Remember that Satan is behind it all.
      1. He knows how to get us.
         a. Through our strong point.
         b. Through our weak point.
   B. Every time we give in, it means more trouble next time.

III. **How to Meet Temptation.**
   A. Scripture (1 Cor. 10:13).
   B. Flee it (as Joseph did).
   C. Avoid it.
   D. Stand in faith (as Jesus did).
   E. Don't entertain it.
   F. Pick the right company.
   G. Remember Jesus is praying for you.

III. **Summary—How to Remember These Points.**
   A. Promise.
   B. Provision.
   C. Power.
   D. Prayer.

V. **What To Do If You Fail.**
   A. Confess your sin and try again.

500 BIBLE SUBJECTS

THE THREE SALVATIONS

Ephesians 2:4-5; Philippians 2:12,13; Romans 13:11

I. **There Is a Past, a Present, and a Future Tense When We Conjugate the Word "Saved." The believer *has been saved*, *is being saved*, and *is to be saved*.**

    A. Salvation means deliverance—deliverance from some kind of danger or evil.

        1. In the first text it means deliverance from the *guilt of sin*.

        2. In the second from the *power of sin*.

        3. In the third from the *penalty of sin*.

    B. These three deliverances include pardon, sanctification and glorification.

        1. Pardon does not include sanctification, nor do these two include the third.

        2. Each blessing is distinct from the others.

    C. We are not to rest content with the first, as we are too apt to do.

    D. Do you want the second, for deliverance from the thrall, the bondage of sin?

II. **Let Us Examine More Carefully These Three Salvations.**

    A. The deliverance from *Guilt*.

        1. "There is no condemnation to them that are in Christ Jesus." To the penitent one Jesus said, "Thy sins be forgiven thee." In that sense, child of God, you have already been saved.

        2. But Jesus added, "Go, and sin no more."

And this brings us to the thought in the second text, namely,

    B. Deliverance from the *Power of Sin*.

    C. And what of the future hereafter?

        1. "It doth not yet appear."

        2. "We shall be like Him."

        3. "He shall change these vile bodies."

        4. "When He shall appear a second time without sin unto salvation."

III. **There Is to Be a Final and Glorious Deliverance From the Power of Death and the Grave, and This Deliverance, this salvation, "is nearer than when we first believed."**

F. B. MEYER

THE WARNING ARROWS

1 Samuel 20:22

I. **The Story of the Arrows of the Text.**
It is an episode in the life of David. Saul's hatred of the young warrior. Jonathan's love for him. The stratagem for giving warning to the hidden David.

II. **Quivers That Are Full of Warning Arrows.**
   A.   The Bible is one of these quivers.
   It is full of these arrows. "The soul that sinneth," etc. "Whatsoever a man soweth," etc. "So then everyone of us shall give," etc.
   B.   Every Gospel minister is such a quiver.
   In olden times ministers were "hell-fire preachers." Why? Not popular to do so now. But the minister must warn.
   C.   The providences of God in daily life are such quivers.
   The daily press furnishes the materials out of which to make these arrows. The embezzler, unfaithful trustee, dishonest politician, every wrongdoer's story.

III. **What These Warning Arrows Signify.**
   A.   These arrows signify present danger.
   That was the way Jonathan put his sign. The dam, the little water trickling through. "Condemned already."
   B.   These arrows signify the greatest friendship.
   Jonathan's interest in David was at the peril of his life. Jesus says, "Am I your enemy?" etc. What friendship cost Him.
   C.   These arrows signify a way of escape.
   In David's case the arrow said, "Go thy way." What is the way from eternal ruin? It is only through Jesus.

IV. **A Word to Those for Whose Sake These Arrows Are Shot.**
   Don't delay, delays are dangerous.
                                    SKETCHES OF REVIVAL SERMONS